D0446124

decentralized

Also by Bo Chancey

I'm Going to Light Myself on Fire

Pray for One

Every Day with Jesus

What's Your Problem

Another Day with Jesus

Don't Say "$#%&X" in Church!

I Hate the Zoo

Find these and other titles at amazon.com.

decentralized

bo chancey

PRESS

Copyright © 2019 by Bo Chancey

First Edition
10 9 8 7 6 5 4 3 2

Unless otherwise indicated, all scripture quotations are taken from the HOLY BIBLE, NEW INTERNATIONAL VERSION®. NIV®. Copyright© 1973, 1978, 1984, 2011 by Biblica, Inc.™ Used by permission. All rights reserved.

All rights reserved. Published by 41Press. No part of this publication may be reproduced, stored in a retrieval system or transmitted, in any form or by any means - electronic, mechanical, photocopying, recording or otherwise - without prior written permission.

For information or bulk sales contact:
Manchester Christian Church
56 Old Bedford Road, Bedford, NH 03110

office@manchesterchristian.com

ISBN: 978-0-9968757-4-5

CONTENTS

The Church is a river.

It cuts a wide berth through history, and the current is gaining strength.

The Church is fluid. It is living water; it is not stagnant.

It is a wild river that cannot be contained.

There are tributaries, streams, creeks, pools and waterfalls to explore.

They are all different expressions of the same river.

This river has a beginning and an end.

It has a source and a destination.

Jesus is our beginning and end. He is our source and our destination.

Jesus' Church flows ever deeper, ever wider and ever wilder.

eᴏ

1

out of the box

Stop thinking about church as a box.

Church leaders have preached for generations that the church is not a building, religious expression or denomination. The Church is people.

The sermons repeat: "The church is not a building. The church is not a building. The church is not a building."

But then every activity and ministry effort is building-reliant. Even outreach efforts are basically nothing more than gimmicks designed to get new people into the building.

"Come to church. Be at church. Don't miss church."

Church is boxed up into centralized experiences and activities that are separate from everyday living. How can people actually **be** the Church when they are so busy going **to** the church?

It is not difficult to understand how this type of thinking became normative.

Large investments are made into building bigger and bigger church boxes. The boxes are more than just buildings—they are the institutions, denominations, hierarchies, structures, traditions and methods that we use to express and share our religious inclinations. Christianity is packaged and placed on shelves for the consumer to come and pick up their faith-in-a-box.

We traded Jesus' model of "go and be" for a consumer model of "come and receive."

Knowledge is power. The more educated people become, the less likely they will be oppressed. Things like literacy, access to information and freedom of expression are primary factors in toppling oppressive power structures.

The Dark Ages represent a period in history where the Church held significant power and control over people. The message of Jesus became increasingly perverted and diluted until it was essentially unrecognizable. The construct for church (the box) was used to enslave people instead of to empower people.

Then this wonderful invention called the printing press came on the scene. Books could be mass-produced, and the mass production of books allowed for mass consumption of information. Access to information sparked a rise in literacy and educational opportunities which generated new ways of thinking to challenge the existing strongholds.

Ordinary people outside of the confines of the box could read the Bible for themselves and ask intelligent questions. They could share their discoveries with people through the dissemination of printed materials that people could access anywhere at any time. The Protestant Reformation exploded out of this new age of enlightenment.

It was an exciting and terrifying time. Change was coming fast, but it was not cheap. Can you imagine being a part of breaking free from the stranglehold of darkness that engulfed centuries of people? Regular, common people could finally rebel against oppression. It happened in the church, in government and in social constructs.

Right now, we are in a period of history that is more pivotal than the Protestant Reformation. The internet changes everything. People can learn as much as they want as fast as possible. Information is shared instantly, and innovations are exploding all around us. This pace of change would be unimaginable to someone living only fifty years ago.

The powerful computers we carry around in our pockets empower us to think, question, share and change. For instance, while reading this chapter, you may start to wonder about the Dark Ages and the Protestant Reformation. Awesome...you do not need me to provide you with an extensive breakdown and commentary on that historical period. I am able to casually reference it (and even overly simplify it) because you can read and discuss it on your own for as long as you like. I paused while writing to do a quick online search and ended up reading twelve articles in under an hour.

Access to information changes our consumer needs. The church box model is changing right before our eyes. This is terrifying for those who believe that their methodology for church is actually the Church. We often come to love our expressions of church more than we love Jesus and His kingdom.

This is why the church can be so slooooooooooooooooooooow to change. Much of our current methodology is derived from needs that were felt half a century ago.

The primary purpose of church was to give people information about the Bible. The only way to give them this information was to have them come to a centralized place (a box...a building) and listen to the only person in town who had access to the information. Essentially, you had one guy who went to school or seminary with access to books who could acquire knowledge and then teach his flock what he knew.

People had no other access to this information. They were reliant on a singular voice and had to go to a singular place. This is why most churches placed such a high priority on attendance. People had to be there every Sunday morning, Sunday night and Wednesday night. It was important not to miss because the teaching was building on itself. If you missed a session, you would get left behind in the teaching. This was the only access a regular person had to the information.

The life of the church essentially revolved around information dissemination. The church building was where you had to go in order to learn about God. Denominations were crucial so that people could have some confidence that they were getting the proper "spin" on their tri-weekly information downloads. Seminaries were vital so that you could check your teacher's credentials. Insanely long doctrinal statements became normative so that every question was settled by the educated authorities, and there was no mystery left to be explored or questioned on your own. Favored church expressions were heavily academic-based.

The centralized, come-to-our-building model was the only way to deliver the information. It was an appealing model to people with a modern mindset. The modern mindset desired information, required evidence and loved proofs. The thinking was "prove it to me, so I can believe it" and "feed me information, so I can believe it more." Modern thinkers often valued information over experience.

Post-modern thinking evolved as our access to information increased. Information did not decrease in importance, but our ability to quickly find answers anywhere and anytime, combined with the continual bombardment of information flowing at us incessantly, changed our felt needs. Post-modern thinkers typically value experience over information. They do not necessarily need more data to believe. They want to see it in action and feel the experience of being a part of it.

The internet is changing the ways we think and interact with our world. It does not matter whether you think the changes are good or bad. What matters is that we recognize the changes and adapt.

If we do not adapt, we will become irrelevant.

Consider how one-on-one conversations have changed. I remember being on a road trip and having a conversation with my Dad about sports. He mentioned a player who held the NFL record for the longest field goal. He could not remember the player's name, and he asked me if I knew. I responded that I could see a picture of him in my mind and I remembered that he only had half his right foot and wore a special shoe to kick with, but I could not remember his name. Our conversation was on pause while we both tried to remember that guy's name. We were stuck because the name was on the tip or our tongues, and neither of us would move on until we had that name.

That was when I looked at my Dad and said, "If we only had a device that would allow us to access information about anything from anywhere at any time."

I pulled out my phone and fifteen seconds later said, "Tom Dempsey…63-yard field goal for the Saints against the Lions on November 8, 1970!"

Dad said, "Yeah…Dempsey." Then we proceeded to have a conversation about overcoming obstacles and how sometimes our handicaps can become strengths.

The information mattered. We were honestly stuck without it. What changed is our access to the information. We can find, share and apply information on the fly. We do not have to memorize everything, own volumes of books, drive to a library or have experts on speed dial.

If we do not adapt,
we will become
irrelevant.

It is still fun to try to remember things, but it is more of a pastime than a necessity. I love playing the game Trivial Pursuit. A buddy and I play almost every Friday morning. It is fun to think about questions, make mental connections, recall information and give educated guesses. It is fun but not needed. My friend and I find ourselves studying for Trivial Pursuit. We watch classic films that we otherwise might ignore. We read articles on a wide range of topics. When we get a question that we know nothing about, we do a quick online search and discover more.

Trivial Pursuit puts out new versions of cards almost every year, but the only version we will play with is the original 1981 edition. The game is about nostalgia for us, and we enjoy the added challenge of remembering that all of the answers are pre-1981. We are Trivial Pursuit snobs that refuse to play with lesser opponents, mock new versions and follow strict house rules for our game play.

We are like a lot of churches. We enjoy our game our way and do not care about the changing world around us. It does not matter to us that many of the answers to the 1981 version are incorrect. Some are outdated. Like, who holds the NFL record for the longest field goal? The answer on the 1981 version is Tom Dempsey, but the actual answer is Matt Prater. He kicked a 64-yard field goal in 2013. Some of the answers in the 1981 version are based on urban-legend and are simply false. Like, Otto Titzling did not invent the brassiere, and Thomas Crapper did not invent the flush toilet. Both of those are funny but ultimately wrong answers to questions. We actually enjoy arresting our mental development to think in terms of pre-1981 scientific discoveries and perceptions of the known world.

Pursuing trivia is more trivial than ever before. This is especially true in churches.

Most church expressions love pre-1981 methodology. I am referring to much, much more than musical style and ministry methodology. A lot of us think that our churches are pretty hip because we have rocking bands for worship, kicking sound and lights, a humorous preacher who utilizes props, a system of small groups that meet in homes, an up-to-date website, a social media presence and all the bells and whistles of a truly modern church. Yep…we keep building boxes for the modern church in a post-modern world. All of that hip methodology still centers on a centralized system of information dissemination. "Come to our box to get the information you need."

When a church sees its primary mission as delivering information to its members, then it only stands to reason that over time the information shared will become increasingly trivial. The gospel is simple. The Bible is simple. Orthodox doctrine is simple.

Jesus summed it all up with two commands that are really one. Love God and love people.

Churches complicate things just like the legal experts in Jesus's day. Those experts in the Law were called Pharisees. Their job was to interpret, apply and enforce 613 Old Testament Laws. It was a heavy burden. Jesus came to take care of that burden for us. He said, "Come to me all you who are weary, and I will give you rest."

Love God. Love people. Go make disciples.

Simply, that's the required information. Everything beyond that is increasingly trivial.

I find it amusing when Christian people talk about deep sermons. They want biblical depth in the preaching they listen to, but what they consider to be "deep" is typically "shallow." Bible trivia is not deep.

Love God. Love People. Make disciples. That is DEEP!

Exploring the subtle nuances of scripture can be fun and useful for sharpening the mind, but do not confuse it with depth. Simple is not shallow and complex is not deep. Complexity creates a greater possibility of being superficial. Jesus called the Pharisees whitewashed tombs and dirty dishes. He said that they were all sparkly on the outside but were dead and nasty on the inside. Doesn't that seem like what a lot of our churches become?

When a church sees its primary purpose as delivering information, the information shared will become increasingly more obscure and trivial in order to keep the consumers coming back. The person delivering the information must retain his/her position as the expert by feeding people things they do not already know. People find themselves eight levels removed from the deep truth of who God is and who we are in relation to Him and believing that some irrelevant tidbit of Bible trivia is deep.

I have preached sermons where long-time church attenders have approached me afterward to tell me how much they loved the deep parts of my preaching. Whenever I ask them what they mean by deep, they always respond by referencing some side comment about the history or context of the biblical text. Most people have come to believe that Bible trivia is deep preaching.

The deepest thing I have ever said or will ever say is, "Love God, love people, go and make disciples."

Trivia can be fun. I appreciate it more than most. Let's just make sure we don't confuse trivia with a deep relationship with Jesus.

Love God.
Love People.
Make disciples.

That is DEEP!

Sometimes when I preach, I provide a piece of trivia, and I can see that it excites churchy people (while at the same time overwhelming new people), so I will stop and explain. I will say something like, "That information is pretty cool. You guys are probably impressed that I knew that information. I am, after all, the expert in this room, and I just demonstrated my expertise by teaching you something new. You should be amazed by my breadth of knowledge. Do you know how I discovered that information? It was not through years of study or intense scholastic discipline. I did a web search an hour ago on the topic, and what I told you was in the first paragraph of the first article that came up."

Access to information changes what we deliver in our churches. People are literate, and they have access to free Bibles. A phone with a Bible app provides more information than a lifetime of sermons ever could. Access to information allows people to *be* the Church instead of spending all their energy going to church.

Church expressions must shift from information dissemination to creating experiences that people can share with others. Worship gatherings are important, but the primary purpose is not information dissemination. We gather to experience God's presence and to respond to Him by exalting Him in worship. God is revealed through the worship of His people. Followers of Jesus will excitedly bring people with them to these gatherings because they have great confidence that their friends, family, neighbors and co-workers will encounter the presence of the living God and have the opportunity to surrender their lives to Him. Preaching good news is a vital part of the worship gathering as it reminds us why we worship and celebrate. Preaching offers an invitation to all to respond to God's presence by yielding to Him. Communal gatherings allow people to celebrate God together and provoke people to pursue God in everyday living.

Is it necessary for people to be present every week in a church building to accomplish this? Dare I even ask the question?

I have asked the question, and the answer is a resounding "NO."

We have damaged people by teaching them to go to church instead of **go and be** the Church. We round them up in our boxes to protect and hold onto our flocks. We guilt and manipulate in the name of Jesus to keep them coming back for more. Why?

I hate how enslaved churchy people sometimes are. Sometimes I run into people who are a part of our church, but they have not attended for a few weeks. They see me, and their expressions quickly move from shock to embarrassment. They explain that they have not been to church for a while, and they apologize profusely. I tell people the same thing every time this happens. "What are you apologizing for? I love our worship gatherings. They have been great experiences that I am sure you would have enjoyed. You might have missed out on something cool, but there is nothing to apologize for. What have you guys been up to?"

They then tell me about their lives and what they have been doing. I encourage them in those activities to be the Church. Be the Church in your home, in your travels, in your hobbies, in your work and in everything you do. Institutionalized guilt melts away when you remind people that Jesus is about us being His Church instead of going to church.

Access changes everything. People can sing worship songs and watch sermons from anywhere at any time. They can do it in cars in the parking lot at their kid's soccer game. They can do it in tents on a mountainside while on a family camping trip. They can do it in a coffee shop, a living room, an airplane, around the dinner table, at work, in a hospital and so on.

More worship services in more places allows us to reach the most people in the shortest time. Worship services no longer require a box. We are free to worship in Spirit and in Truth.

In John 4, Jesus has an encounter with a Samaritan woman at a well. She asked Him a religious question regarding where people had to go to worship. The Jews worshiped at the Temple in Jerusalem and the Samaritans worshiped on a mountain, and she wanted to know who was religiously correct.

Religion is all about the rules for worship...where, when and how. It boxes worship up and presents it as a confined experience. Jesus did not come to start a new religion. Jesus came to set us free from our boxes.

Jesus told the Samaritan woman that the time had come for true worshipers to worship in Spirit and in Truth.

Jesus is the truth. Worship is centered on Him.

The Spirit is free. He moves like the wind. He cannot be contained. He cannot be boxed in.

True worshipers will worship Jesus everywhere all the time in every way. Worship is not relegated to scheduled times in static locations. For a long time, this type of thinking has been applied only on individualized terms. Churches may teach that people can have one-on-one worship experiences anywhere at any time, but communal worship must happen in set places at set times. It is not true anymore. We now have decentralized communal worship opportunities.

The reach and impact of the local church really can extend to the very ends of the earth. We are alive in the most exciting time for the gospel. The Church is unleashed. We are no longer limited by our physical resources. Growth is not limited by the number of seats in the building or spots in the parking lot. Reach is not defined by a ten-minute-drive perimeter. Churches do not need to compete with busyness, youth sports, work schedules, pretty days, rainy days, snowy days, sad days, holidays or any days because we can have worship services every day.

∾

2

into the air

Does online worship count?

Count for what? And who is counting?

Do you want to know who resists online worship the most? Satan.

The Devil is working overtime to keep people boxed up in religious expressions. As long as the Church stays put in their little church buildings, Satan is happy. But a Decentralized Church is free to move into enemy territory to set the captives free. The Devil is freaking out over this new reality, and he is working overtime to throw local churches into confusion and disarray over this amazing opportunity.

The Devil is a deceiver, and he is good at what he does.

People are entrenched in their religious expressions, and they will fight to maintain what they believe is the right way to worship. They make fine-sounding arguments that others easily accept as truth, but a little questioning and prodding reveals that the arguments are mostly fear-based attempts to avoid change.

The first comment I often hear is a quote from scripture. "Do not give up meeting together as some are in the habit of doing."

2,000 years ago, physically meeting together was the only way to share information. Gathering together at a specific time in a specific place was the most efficient way to connect with people. You could not make a phone call to ask a question or share some news. You could not send an email, and even if you could, very few people were literate. One of the great errors of the Church over the centuries has been the creation of an artificial community that pulls people out of their organic communities.

Satan licks his chops at the thought of Christians huddled together in church buildings isolated and insulated from their world. Satan has no problem with people going to church, so long as they never really are the Church. What if we prioritized our time differently, and people could receive the same content with greater retention in half the time?

The typical Sunday church experience does not actually allow for much relational connectivity. I know…I know….*your* church is different. You serve donuts and coffee between your first and second service so that people can hang out and really get to know one another. Is that really what is happening, or is your church just getting fatter while having fake conversations over bad coffee? I'm not accusing. I'm just asking the question. Perhaps you think your church is different because you have a minute after the first worship song for people to shake hands and say hello. Sure…nothing builds authentic community like an awkward handshake and a pretend smile.

I have preached in churches of all shapes and sizes, and the truth of the matter is that there is not much relational connectivity happening during the worship gatherings. Most worship services are static environments where people sit quietly and listen. They cannot really ask questions or discuss what is happening. They come and go without much occurring other than fulfilling a religious obligation.

Why?

Consider the time that is spent for the average family to get to a church service. They must wake up on Sunday morning, have breakfast, get dressed, load up the car, drive to the church building, find a parking spot, check the kids into the children's ministry and then find a seat. No wonder most families fight on Sunday mornings. For years, pastors have blamed spiritual warfare for the frustrating dynamic of getting a family to Sunday worship on time, but it seems to me to be more of a natural reaction to an unnatural activity.

Take the one day of the week that people do not have to run around like crazy and convince them to run around like crazy in order to meet their religious obligations. What in the world are we doing to people?

I am not proposing that we abandon worship gatherings in set locations at set times, but I am suggesting that we think differently about how often people will be physically present. I believe that communal worship experiences are more crucial now than ever before, and I think that we ought to offer more services in more places at more times. We just should not expect everyone to be there every week. I also think that in many cases it is better that they are not physically present every week in a church building.

A family that worships together in their living room and has the opportunity to discuss what they are experiencing in real time is a powerful thing. An individual sitting in a coffee shop with a laptop and headphones can utilize the chat feature to ask questions, share prayer requests, answer questions and pray for others. That is a powerful thing. Someone taking the time they otherwise would have spent getting ready for church, driving to church, going into church, leaving church and driving home from church and instead using it for rest, recreation, family time, serving other or just about anything besides sin is a powerful thing.

Online worship opportunities are powerful.

An argument that many people make in response to this is to ask what if people just watch online and do not really participate. Great question. I will answer that question with a question. How is that any different from people showing up at a building, sitting in the back row, blending in and sneaking out during the last song?

Maybe you are thinking, "We would never allow that to happen at our church." Really? If that is true, then I bet you do not have a lot of new people showing up and that most who do never come back. Churches that really love people allow them to try things out and experience worship at their own pace. They are available to answer questions, make connections and help meet needs, but they are not pushy.

I was skeptical of online worship until I experienced it firsthand in a variety of contexts. I watched services alone in peace and quiet. I was able to really rest and focus on God while being refreshed. I watched alone and actively engaged with the chat features, online connect card and the host. It was fun interacting with others while the service was going on. We were asking questions and answering one another in real time. We were even sharing links to other sermons and websites, so we could explore that day's topic further. I was energized by the experience. I worshiped with my family online, and we laughed together, sang together and discussed the sermon...all while still in our pajamas!

But the thing that really put me over the top with online worship experiences happened one weekend when my travel plans changed unexpectedly. We have a Thursday night worship service that is recorded each week and serves as a backup for our video-based campuses. I had preached that Thursday on the topic of family and how God provides hope for all of our dysfunctional, broken family dynamics. I was scheduled to fly to Florida for a conference on Sunday afternoon, but a blizzard was going to hit our city on Saturday night. I decided to get out ahead of the storm and flew to Florida on Saturday morning.

Since I was going to have an extra night in Florida, I called a friend who had moved there and asked if he would like to hang out. He invited me to spend the night at his home, and I eagerly accepted. This particular friend was someone I had prayed for, and he had recently become a follower of Jesus. He had moved to Florida for health reasons but was actively worshiping with our church online.

Online worship opportunities are powerful.

When I arrived at his home on Saturday night, I was surprised that he gave me his bedroom and that he was going to sleep on the couch. I knew that there was another bedroom and asked why he did not have me sleep there. My friend explained that he had another friend who had come into town unexpectedly, and that friend was sleeping in the spare bedroom. I offered to get a hotel room, but my friend insisted that I stay. He explained that his friend was someone that he was praying for, and the friend was having family troubles. He felt like us being there at the same time was no coincidence. God's timing, so to speak.

We woke up on Sunday morning, and I met my friend's friend. We were hanging out in the living room, drinking coffee when our host announced that it was time for church. He turned the TV on, and there was our church…live online in his living room in Florida. We sang a little, talked about our church a little and listened to the music a little. When it came time for the sermon, I could feel them both stare at me when my face came on the TV screen. We were showing the recorded sermon from Thursday night. I smiled and said, "I've seen this one already…it's a good one."

They laughed, and we listened to me preach. There were a couple of times where I said something in the sermon that struck me as powerful as I listened. I said something to the guys like, "That was good…I need to remember that and put it into practice." We started commenting on different thoughts and scripture from the message and even paused it at one point to talk a little more. As the sermon was wrapping up, my host got up and went into the kitchen. He came back with communion for all of us. We shared communion, and then my friend said, "Let's go get breakfast."

We went to a breakfast spot not far from the house and talked about Jesus, life and family struggles for the next two hours. It was one of the best church experiences of my entire life! We had a preacher, a new follower of Jesus and someone who was exploring a relationship with Jesus all worshiping together and sharing real life. I was 2,000 miles away from our church building and was with only two other people instead of the thousands that were physically present in our buildings, but the experience was superior.

I decided then and there to never discount online worship again. It is powerful and effective. We can reach more people in more places faster than ever.

I understand that there are many questions swirling around this shift in how people consume and participate in what we call church. There is fear, doubt and even anger regarding what has already occurred and the looming changes coming over the horizon. Many doomsday prognosticators are claiming doom and gloom for the future of the Church. I personally believe that is ridiculous. We are moving into what will be the most fruitful era in history for the Church.

Let's address some of the questions regarding online church.

I will begin with one that nobody will ask but is a major part of the conversation.

WHAT ABOUT THE MONEY?

Oh yeah, I went there. What about the money? Church is a business. It is much, much more than a business, but it is still a business. People get bent out of shape when churches make business decisions, but that is the basic reality of how they function in our world. Churches have mortgages, light bills, payroll and many other financial obligations. We can pretend all we want that churches are not businesses, but at the end of the day every church has business concerns that must be addressed

How does online worship impact the business of the church? Some people have asked this question a bit less eloquently. They basically wonder out loud about all the free-loaders online who do not financially support the church. How could they give if there is no obligatory offering plate drifting beneath their noses each week?

Umm…yeah…people do not give via offering plates any more. That is outdated methodology.

I was sitting at a round table of pastors at a conference discussing this topic and meeting a ton of resistance. They were all telling me that passing an offering plate was crucial for their churches. I called a timeout and did a little experiment with them.

I said: "Ok…there is a family in need right outside of this room. They are a great family, and all they need is a few hundred bucks to get them back on their feet. God wants us to help them. God is clearly commanding us to help them. We want to help them. So, let's take up an offering. Everyone take out your wallets and purses. Let's see how much we can come up with right now to meet the need before us."

I seriously made everyone take out their wallets to look inside. There were ten of us around that table, and all told we had $47 in cash, and nobody had a check with them. I told them that we could pass a plate around our table all day long, but it would not matter. Times have changed. Offering plates are goofy now, and people know it. They see those empty plates going by, and it is a foreshadowing of the empty seats they are beginning to see all around them in our church buildings. Churches are ridiculously slow in changing methodology, and it hurts them.

So back to the money question. How does online worship impact the church financially?

The vast majority of people are completely comfortable using money online. We are over the hump of being fearful about putting credit card and bank information into online accounts. This is not an obstacle for the church. People will give online, and it is better.

Why is it better? Because they can make a giving plan, set up their giving to reoccur and never miss out on the joy of giving since it is automatic. Do you remember when churches gave their people 52 offering envelopes a year? Those envelopes were a tool to help people give consistently and to recognize if they missed a week. Online giving is even better.

People who worship online still give to their church. Another thought to consider when thinking about the financial implications of online worship is that the cost per person being reached drops dramatically. Churches that embrace online worship can reach more people for far less money. From a business standpoint, online worship is a smart tool to invest in and encourage. With less giving dollars going to support church infrastructure, there are more dollars available for outreach, community support and global missions.

Yikes! As long as the church tries to fight culture, we will never win people to Christ. Refusing to adapt methodology is just as sinful as telling people to their faces to go to Hell. Churches that love their methodology more than reaching people have become some of the most useful tools in Satan's toolbox.

If our job is to reach the world for Christ, then wouldn't we want to make the gospel as accessible as possible? Rejecting online worship is about as foolish as keeping the Catholic mass in Latin. Hey…let's use a dead language to talk about a dead god to a bunch of dead people in a dead environment. It is more than foolish—it is downright sinful.

Woe to every church that becomes an obstacle to people entering into the kingdom of heaven. It would be better for us to have a millstone tied around our necks and be cast into the sea. If we are not going to change our methodology, the least we could do is die quick deaths so that we are out of the way.

I have already addressed this question a bit anecdotally by sharing how the opportunities for organic, authentic community are actually greater with online worship than going to a building to worship. There are of course no guarantees that people will engage in community. They may still decide not to connect, but I sense a greater freedom and better connectivity will occur.

If we stop driving people to buildings to experience community and instead equip them for Christ-honoring relationships in the places they already live, work and play, then I think we are on to something powerful. Many of our attempts at small-group connections have actually removed people from the communities into which God had strategically placed them. When we teach people to come to a church group, ministry or activity, we must also realize the possibility that we are removing them from something else. That can be good or bad. We might be replacing a sinful activity with a church activity, but we might also be replacing authentic community with a manufactured sense of community.

We end up reinforcing the idea of going to church instead of being the church. How many people do we have serving in our churches who would never serve anyone in their homes or at work? It is disgusting.

Online worship reinforces the reality that we are the Church wherever we are. This transforms the ways we interact with people in the environments we already live in. Christ-centered community can blossom anywhere and everywhere as people focus on being the Church instead of going to church. Authentic community can flourish as we share our lives with people we interact with on a regular basis.

How often is church community phony? Think about the rules of church buildings. Don't cuss in church. Don't lie in church. Don't run in church. We treat our church buildings like they are holy places for holy people. Be whatever you want outside of these walls, but when you are here act holy. All of that acting and pretending in church buildings negatively impacts the possibility of godly community. For good reason, people are hesitant to share what they actually think, feel and experience.

Online worship allows people to ask for prayer, pray for others, pose questions and share answers in real time. It reminds people to be the Church wherever they are and creates greater access to community.

What about accountability?

Allowing people to be and experience church anywhere anytime increases accountability. Our boxed church methodologies often treat church like activities that you participate in from time to time as opposed to a 24/7 reality. The best accountability you can have is to remember that you are the Church. We are Christ's Body...His physical presence on earth. What we do is what He does, and what we do not do is what He does not do.

There is gravity to knowing who you fully are in Christ. You pay closer attention to how you think, what you say and what you do. You move from acting like a Christian a couple of times a week to living out a transformed identity. Every place becomes sacred and holy to us because worship is not confined to a building. This renewed mindset helps hold us accountable to yield to the work of the Holy Spirit within us.

As worship moves out of the box and into the air, we recognize that every place is sacred, and every relationship can be Christ-centered. If I am centered in Christ—if He is my core identity—then my relationships will be transformed. I am carrying Jesus into every conversation and activity. I am mindful that He is present, in fact, just as mindful as if I was in a building full of people singing worship songs.

People respect this kind of living. They are intrigued and helpful. Most of the time, they hold onto you in order to be lifted up, not to drag you down. Traditional church teaching drills into us that the world is trying to drag us down. I have discovered the opposite. People want to be lifted up, but our boxed church expressions have made them feel left out.

The best accountability is not necessarily found in a holy huddle but in down and dirty relationships. I know a lot of churches encourage people to have accountability partners. The idea is basically to get people paired up with someone who once a week will ask "the tough questions." I am in no way opposed to this type of accountability, but let's think about the dynamic. People are asking tough questions that they do not know the answers to. They will not have any evidence to know whether or not the other person is telling the truth. These people are not really doing life together. If they were, the questions would not need to be asked.

The best accountability happens with people we encounter every day. Participating in a small group or calling an accountability partner can be supplemental, but it must not take the place of being accountable to the world we represent Jesus in every day. When you have worship services in your home, you tend to be more mindful that your home is a holy place. When you use your computer, table, cell phone and TV for worship you begin to utilize them differently all of the time. When you worship in your car, you begin to drive differently. When we stop thinking of church as a place to go to and accept that we are the Church, accountability will naturally and supernaturally skyrocket. We think differently about the way we live, and we are accountable in every relationship.

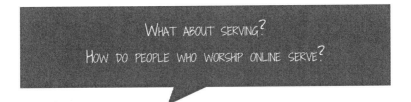

WHAT ABOUT SERVING?

HOW DO PEOPLE WHO WORSHIP ONLINE SERVE?

This one makes me laugh a little. I understand the question. I wrestled with it myself, but having come out on the other side, I can now see the absurdity of it.

Churches inadvertently taught people that serving Jesus means volunteering at a church building. We know that this is not true. We know that "servant" is more of an identity than an activity, but our boxed church expressions repeatedly ask people to serve at the church more often than encouraging people to be servants everywhere they go.

Local churches are often full of greeters, aisle hosts, parking lot attendants, children's teachers, lay leaders, musicians and behind-the-scenes volunteers who faithfully serve Jesus at the church building but never serve Him anywhere else. They serve at church but not at home or work or in the community. For many church attenders, servanthood starts and stops at the doors of a church building. It is sad, yet we keep reinforcing this kind of thinking each time we encourage people to serve and then rattle off the serving opportunities available within the walls of the church building.

Here is the kicker…if everyone who attends our church tried to serve at our church, we would not have enough volunteer positions for everyone, and they know it.

Let's say that our children's ministry needs twelve new volunteers to serve each week, and the team is struggling to recruit. I am not about to stand up in front of thousands of people and ask for people to serve in that ministry. It is silly and ineffective. People assume someone else is more qualified or more interested or has a greater desire. They think, "They don't really need me," and they are correct. We do not need every single person serving in ministries within the church, but the kingdom does require every follower of Jesus to be servants everywhere.

Online worship helps me remember that truth. When addressing our church (online and those in one of our buildings), I encourage them to be servants instead of pushing specific serving activities. In addition to holding a deeper understanding of servanthood, there are ways that people serve online. Our online campus has volunteer hosts, people praying, troubleshooters who are watching and fixing technical glitches and so on.

The ability to have worship services anywhere at any time changes the way we think about serving. If online is where you worship, it stands to reason that you might be more likely to serve Jesus when you are online. If you worship in your home, it stands to reason that you might be more likely to serve Jesus in your home. Serving moves from being a static activity to a living identity.

Getting worship out of the box and into the air releases the church to be the Church. It is an answer to the fervent prayers of generations of people who longed for a day when people could understand that the Church is not a building...The Church is people. We are temples of the Holy Spirit, and the true worshipers of God worship in Spirit and in truth.

eOo

3

the real world

Okay…this is the DON'T FREAK OUT CHAPTER!

Breathe. It is going to be alright. It will be better than alright. It will be amazing.

This is not the end of Christianity but a new beginning fit for a changing world. Online worship may not be your cup of tea, and you may avoid technology at all costs, but the internet is impacting every church.

It was not too long ago that people ridiculed online dating sites. Those sites were the punchlines to jokes. I remember the first time someone told me that they met their spouse online, and they were not joking. I was, like, "Oh. You are serious…you guys actually did meet online, and you are not embarrassed by that."

Now, the most common answer I get to the "how did you meet" question is…online. What once seemed ridiculous and like a short-term fad became completely normal. Why? Because it works. Online dating is efficient and effective.

I often hear people say that the internet is not the real world. That is a strange sentiment that is rapidly evaporating. We interact with real people, buy real products, spend real money, consume real information and experience real entertainment in real time. The internet is often far more real than our interactions in the physical world.

Consider online dating. What is more real…dressing up, going to a nightclub, putting out the vibe and hoping to catch a mate or scrolling through profiles looking for common interests and beginning written correspondence from the comfort of your own home? Are you more likely to make good decisions in a crowded, smoke-filled bar with music blaring and the lights dimmed low or from behind a computer screen where you can ask clearer questions and evaluate the responses over as much time as you like with whoever you like?

The reality of internet connections impacts the purpose and functionality of nightclubs and bars. These establishments continue to exist, but the way people utilize them is changing. They used to be places where people would go to meet new people. Now they are places where people go to meet up with people they already know. They used to all be super similar with few variations in atmosphere, music and drink offerings. Now they are becoming more eclectic… whiskey bars, wine bars, martini bars, microbrew bars, karaoke bars, tequila bars, hookah bars, theme-based bars and so forth. Bars are not necessarily trying to create community. They are providing spaces for people to express community.

Bar hopping is a thing. People will meet up and go out with the intention of hitting several different establishments. There is not a ton of loyalty to a specific bar. Gone are the days of people hanging out at one specific neighborhood watering hole. Access to transportation and increased communication abilities change the ways we engage in community. People do not have to go to a set location and hope that they run into people they know. They can use their cellphones to access social media on the fly, text their friends and have a car pick them up to take them to wherever their peer group is hanging out.

I think this analogy aptly applies to church.

People go to bars for experiences. Alcohol consumption is a completely secondary function of a bar. That is why people gladly pay three times as much for a drink in a bar compared to what it would cost in their homes. They are paying for an experience. Neighborhood bars were places that people could go to after work to see friends and meet new people. Changes in transportation, technology and communications impacted these neighborhood establishments. People are less likely to go to a place where everybody knows their names when they have access to social media in the palms of their hands 24-7.

Any bar that relies on customer loyalty and a neighborhood clientele is in trouble. Those businesses need to cast a wider net to attract a broader base. They must pay attention to details. Things like marketing, signage, a social media presence, cleanliness, lighting, customer service and constant evaluation are all critical if they want to stay in business.

The same is true for the local church.

Providing the information is a secondary function of the local church. People have access to the information and can get it anywhere at any time. Local churches offer an experience. The experience inside a church building is different from an online experience. Arguing about which experience is better is foolish and unproductive. Better or worse is irrelevant…what matters is that both are available, both are useful, and they are not in competition with one another.

If you are fighting against online church expressions, you have already lost. The ship has sailed, and it is barreling full-steam ahead.

Fighting against it is pointless and evil. God is using the internet to save the world just like He used Roman roads, the printing press and traveling tent revivals. It is time to get on board and rethink the expressions of the local church.

Before people had access to transportation and communication, they were essentially bound to their neighborhood churches. Local churches held a steady base of people that were loyal to their denominational expression and geographical identity. This allowed churches to be sloppy without much short-term consequence. They did not need to have great leadership, good programing, excellent experiences, engaging people, updated facilities or new methodologies in order to exist. So, they existed for a time, but existing does not last. Churches that refuse to thrive eventually begin to die.

And die they did. And dying they are.

Churches that do not pay attention to the experience that they are creating will not reach the world they live in. They will end up like those gross, run-down, dark and empty neighborhood bars that nobody wants to go into anymore. Times have changed, so get on with the business of changing or dry up, die out and get out of the way.

What will people experience in your church building that they could not experience more efficiently and effectively online?

The shared experience of being part of the crowd is energizing and encouraging. A church building can be effectively utilized to create that kind of environment. It can also be used to provide a space that feels sacred and works to remove distractions, so people can focus on God's presence. The local church building can be a place to experience a physical connection with the family of God.

I do not think there this a need to eliminate church buildings, but there is a need to be extremely intentional in how we use church buildings.

Technology impacts our felt needs. There are reasons why people are attending worship services in church buildings less frequently. The average committed church attender is going to a building about once a month. I do not think the reason for this trend is that people love Jesus and His Church less. I think it is because people are already engaging with Jesus and His Church more. They do not need a Sunday Jesus fix and a mid-week pick-me-up, because they can watch sermons, read books, listen to podcasts and stream worship music all day every day.

Our felt needs are changing. We want experiences that we can share with others. We long to be a part of something greater than ourselves and the little slice of the world we typically run around in. We are more interested in participating than merely consuming.

If local churches truly love people, they will adapt their methodology to meet the changing needs. Sadly, many leaders love their methodology more than the mission of Jesus, and they allow sacred cows to utterly control them. They milk these methods for as long as possible, but they eventually dry up.

A lady approached me in the lobby on a Sunday morning and expressed that she had to tell me a story. I listened intently as she shared about attending a rummage sale at a local church, and while there, she ended up talking about our church. She said that she had no idea what she told them about our church, but when she was done the people running the rummage sale were all in tears. She apparently told them about a warm clothing drive and Thanksgiving meal that we do for our community each year. They were so excited about what they heard that they told the lady to drive her car up to the front, and they loaded all of the warm clothes from their rummage sale into her car. They asked her to donate them through our church to people in need.

As the lady shared this with me, I noticed that she had a large postcard in her hand from that church. I asked her if she wanted me to write a thank you note to the church for their donation, and she said that was why she brought the card they had given her to me. The church's name and address were on the large promotional postcard. I went into my office right away and wrote that church a thank you note, and I noticed something while addressing the envelope.

The postcard had a label placed on it with the dates for their advent services printed on it. It struck me odd that they would stick a label on every card they handed out, so I investigated. At first, I thought that maybe their denomination had provided marketing materials for all their churches to use and each church was responsible for putting labels in the place for the dates and times for their Christmas services. But when I flipped the card back to the front, it was clear that it was printed specifically for that local church. The church name, address, the theme for their advent series and the specific dates were all on the front.

Then it hit me. I thought surely not, but I had to check. I peeled the right side of the label, and sure enough…it listed the same dates except instead of 2018, it said 2012. The postcard was six-years old and was being recycled.

Some church leaders might think that this was a savvy move on their part. We could think that they were being frugal and wise to hold onto extra cards for six years so as not to waste them. I get that kind of thinking and was actually kind of impressed that they remembered they had them after six years.

Here is the problem…in six years nothing had changed in their church. The theme was the same. The service times were the same. The location was the same. Their methodology was the same. Nothing had changed.

But that is not completely true. Something **had** changed.

When I looked over the card again, I was struck by the sweet picture they used on it. The picture was of a teenage girl holding hands with an elementary aged girl in the church's sanctuary. The church's methodology may not have changed, but I knew that those girls had changed. They had grown up. I wondered what it would be like for them to look at that postcard six years later. Were they still a part of that church? Had they moved away? What would it look like if they recreated the photo?

Churches always change because the church is people, and people are constantly changing. This reason alone ought to be enough to convince churches of the importance of adapting methodology to reach the world around them. Sadly, we are prone to dig our heels in and spin our wheels. We create ruts and get stuck. The world moves on, but we sit still and wonder where everybody went. The two girls in the picture grew up while the church suffered from severe arrested development. Six years without change is shocking, but decades without change is downright sinful.

In order to reach real people in the real world with the real Jesus, we must genuinely change our methodology. We must constantly evaluate the felt needs of people and use our resources to address those needs. Much of old church methodology is attempting to scratch itches that no longer exist. That approach is abrasive and eventually becomes irritating. Churches are insanely ineffective when they irritate their world.

The saddest part is when churches blame the world for the irritation. That is not only foolish, it is cruel. Thinking that, just because methodology used to work, it should always work is ridiculous. Blaming culture because your methodology is no longer relevant is ludicrous. It is not the world's fault that churches avoid change.

Waging war against culture does not make much sense. We are called to fight for people not against them. We need to learn to ask better questions. What do people need? What is effective at engaging people? What are people looking for? What does not work any longer? How can we help?

Ask better questions and listen.

Love people, and do not fall in love with your methodology. Over the years I have had many people tell me how much they love whatever methods our church was using at that time. I always remind them that the methods they love today will likely change tomorrow. Our desire is to help people love Jesus and love the people they encounter every day. We never want to replace love for God and people with a love for church programs, worship expressions and the latest, greatest initiatives.

Churches are notorious for pulling people out of the real world to hunker down in the church world. There are entire discipleship models that are based on the premise of getting people to serve inside church buildings and programs. I regularly hear church leaders express a common sentiment: If we can get people to serve at the church, then we can keep them in the church.

How about releasing people to be the Church in the real world? That sounds better to me than pulling people out of the mission field and into the clubhouse.

I had an encounter with a gentleman in the lobby of one of our buildings on a Sunday between services. I had not seen him in several months, and I was excited he was there. I walked over and said, "Hey, man, great to see you!"

He turned around and looked a little embarrassed. He began to apologize for being gone so much and for having to travel for work.

Ask better
questions and
listen.

I told him I was not worried about that and that I was just thrilled to see him.

I was simply saying hello to a friend I had not seen in a while, but he interpreted the encounter as the Pastor of the church scolding him for not being there more often. YUCK! I wish we could strip the obnoxious religious baggage from people, so they could be free.

The gentleman relaxed a little, and I asked him how his business was going. He lit up and began to tell me about a new employee he had hired. He shared how one day, he felt the Holy Spirit prompt him to share the gospel with the new employee. They were traveling, and he told the other guy that he wanted to talk with him about something very important. The new employee asked his boss to come by his hotel room, and my friend went that very night. He shared the gospel, and sure enough, the guy became a Christian right then and there!

I said, "SWEET!" and gave him a solid high-five.

Then the guy told me that he wanted to get more involved in our church and that he wanted to find a place to serve. It was clear to me that he was saying these things out of some sense of religious obligation. I gave him a confused look and said, "Brother…I am sure that we could find something for you to do around here, but the last thing I would ever want to do would be to pull you out of the real world where you are listening to the Holy Spirit and showing up in hotel rooms to share the gospel."

His face lit up, and he looked free and alive. I told him to keep sharing Jesus in his world and to let me know if there was any way I could help him. I told him this because we must refrain from getting people so busy going to church and serving at church that they have no energy or time to **be** the Church.

The truth of the matter is that churches do not need everyone to serve in their ministries. I understand that recruitment for volunteer positions in churches is always a challenge, but just think about the absurdity of telling an entire group of church attenders that every one of them is needed in some capacity to serve within the local church organization.

There are not enough meaningful tasks for everyone, and deep down, they all know they are not really needed. This is why so many are not compelled to serve within the church. The volunteer work for most churches can be done by about 25% of the people who attend. We need to focus on sending people away from our church buildings to live out their servant identities in the real world.

As the Church becomes more decentralized, we also become more powerful. We have more people in more places at more times sharing the love Jesus in more ways than ever before. Church leaders ought to focus more on helping people be effective for Jesus where they live, work and play instead of trying to get people to do churchy things in churchy places.

My friend who travels for work gives and worships online. His growing business is a ministry. God is using him to reach far more people through his everyday living than he would ever impact through serving inside a church building. It is great to see him when he is in town. It is good to touch base for some encouragement and support. The physical connection is helpful, but it is not essential. He needs to stay the course in order to reach his world…his home, his neighborhood, his employees, his clients.

The virtual connection with our local church empowers him to go further and faster with the gospel. He has tools at his disposal, and he has support in his efforts. He is not alone, and online experiences remind him of that fact.

The internet is the real world. Real people make real connections and do real things all day every day online. If we are serious about the mission of Jesus and truly do want to go into ALL the world, then we will go online. We will decentralize. We will send people instead of holding people. We will change, and the real world will be reached.

∽

4

great expectations

When my wife was pregnant with our first child, someone gave us a book called "What to Expect When You're Expecting" by Heidi Murkoff. It was full of useful information about pregnancy, changes to the woman's body and how to prepare for the birth a baby.

We were thrilled to be pregnant but freaked out about all the unknowns. Change is scary. We knew that starting a family would alter everything, but we still had no idea what to expect. The book helped us explore specific questions and to embrace the magnitude of the situation. We were parents, and life would never be the same.

In a similar fashion, the Church is pregnant. We are giving birth to a new expression of the family of God. The kingdom of

God is going to get bigger fast as the gospel zips through the air to the ends of the earth. I understand that for some, this is an unwanted pregnancy. That saddens me, and I do have a message from the Lord for all those who are fearful and unexcited…suck it up!

It is happening. This new expression of the Church is one diddle that cannot be undid. It is coming, and it is coming fast. Just as the printing press sparked the Protestant Reformation and birthed a new Church expression, the internet is allowing for the conception of a birth that will completely change the world.

To be clear, I believe that we are witnessing the birth of a third expression of the Church. There is the Catholic Church, the Protestant Church and the Decentralized Church. What exactly is this Decentralized Church? That is difficult to pinpoint because I do not have the luxury of perspective or the gift of prophecy. But I know that we are in the midst of it. We are neck-deep in the messiness of change. History will provide a clearer picture of the decentralized expression of the family of God, but for now I can attempt to shed some light on what to expect.

Many church leaders will be fearful.

Change freaks people out. We cannot change the fact that things will change, but we can prepare for change. Those who refuse to change will find the emerging Decentralized Church insanely upsetting.

Fear will come through the realization that power, control and resources will move from institutional hierarchies into the hands of ordinary people. The threat of loss typically leads to fear. Fear is a dominant emotion. When fear sets in, it takes control. Fear makes a terrible god.

Fearful leaders will attack what they do not understand. They will resort to the worst tactics religion affords...guilt and manipulation. When fear sets into the hearts of church leaders, they begin to behave in nasty ways. They seek to hold onto every scrap of power at their disposal. They belittle those they feel threatened by. They teach fear. They spread fear. They lead with fear. They live by fear. And fear will kill them.

I am not making light of this fear. I totally understand and appreciate it. Church leaders build churches that have infrastructures. Those infrastructures require resources. It is so easy to fall into the trap of doing ministry to support the infrastructure. Church leaders carry the responsibility of paying the mortgage, compensating staff members, running programs and generally feeding the machine. There is pressure to keep church members happy because happy church members give the money that is needed to keep things

Many church leaders will be fearful.

going. This cycle can quickly escalate to the point where there is a lordship issue.

Who or what is really leading the church? Is it Jesus or the expressions of church that we believe will keep the regulars attending and giving? Fear is the number one cause of missional drift in local churches. The mission of Jesus to save the world is abandoned and replaced with the mission of saving a little slice of power and control.

Fear brings death, and if the fear goes unchecked, death will come swifter than in the past. It used to be that churches could languish in fearful irrelevance for decades before smoldering out, but things are happening much faster now. People have options. They don't need to be trapped in institutionalized fear. There is no social contract holding them to dying churches. Nostalgia, obligation and merely keeping the doors open are not compelling enough reasons for people to invest their lives in a church. People need vision, and vision demands change!

There is a wonderful solution to the fearful leader problem. It is called LOVE. Love drives out fear. Love is powerful, but love for church buildings, programs and methodology is not a living love. Love for God and love for people are the key. The great commandment reveals the necessity of love. Love the Lord your God and love your neighbor. Love is what God is all about. He is love. It is impossible to serve the God of love when fear has a hold on your heart.

Love compels us to action. Love moves us to change. Love drives us to pursue God's best and to never settle for less. If we love Jesus and love the world He longs to save, we will embrace the power of the Decentralized Church as fear is demolished.

It is going to be messy!

I wish I could write with confidence that Christians would walk through this changing dynamic with class, but sadly, that is not very likely. Some people will freak out and behave poorly. I never want to excuse bad behavior, but it is understandable.

Breaking away from a church expression can be painful. Churches that attempt to hold people instead of sending them will add to the messiness. In-fighting will put some black eyes on the Body of Christ. Some will be repulsed by the messiness and will run away from Jesus. The more prepared we are, the less this will happen.

Mistakes will be made. There will be times when the pendulum swings too far. There will be over-corrections to mistakes from the past. There will be attempts to change things that should not be changed. There will be name-calling, generalizations (perhaps like

It is going to be messy!

There will be a choir of voices instead of soloists.

what I am doing in this book) and refusals to find unity in the family of God.

Change always gets messy. Unfortunately, sometimes the baby gets thrown out with the bathwater. I am sure that there will be times when we ask, "Oh...no...where's the baby?" Do not let the messiness disturb you. God is in control, and His plan to save the world is in full effect. We mess it up from time to time, but the gospel will prevail, the church will emerge, and the whole world will know that there is a God who loves them and has a place in His family for them.

There will be a choir of voices instead of soloists.

People will not be listening to one preacher...they will listen to many preachers. Preachers used to preach other preacher's sermons. That is not going to fly anymore. Why preach someone else's sermon when people can listen to the original version any time they want? People are going to be far less likely to put up with bad preaching when they regularly hear good preaching.

People will not participate in only one local church. They will worship with several. We experienced this in student ministry during the 1990s. We had kids who were actively participating the three or four local churches. One church was the place where kids got saved. One was the church with amazing worship. One was the place to hang out with your friends. One was the place their parents like best. Those teenagers from the 1990s have grown up, and they are still experiencing church like that. No one, single, local church needs to provide for every need. We can work together to encourage unity and wholeness within the Body of Christ.

Decentralization is impacting the way we consume and participate in just about everything. When I was a kid, my mom could tell my dad that she needed to go the bank, and he would have known exactly where she was going. That is not the case anymore. First of all, when was the last time you actually went into a bank? Secondly, how many banks are you currently banking with? I just did a quick count of my banks and between checking, savings, mortgage, auto loans, credit cards and investments, I have at least twelve banks that I am actively banking with.

Why?

The internet. We can open accounts, pay bills and shop interest rates without ever leaving our homes. It is easy to diversify and keep track of everything. We have no need for a singular bank to oversee it all. We can take the best from each bank without losing anything in the process. The same is true with the Decentralized Church. People are not going to experience less. They will experience more with better quality and greater effectiveness.

Physical attendance will decrease as engagement increases.

People attend church services in church buildings less often, but that does not mean they are less committed. Consider online giving. People who have reoccurring giving set up online never miss a scheduled gift. They do not need to go to church to put money in an offering plate. They do not need to find a stamp to mail a check to the church. There is no forgetting. There is no changing your mind because things are looking a little tight that month. Online giving allows for greater engagement.

People do not need to go to church to find out what is going on. They can jump on the church's website or social media pages to get updates and news about upcoming initiatives. They do not need the Sunday announcements to be engaged in the life of the church.

People can get updates and prayer requests via email, text message and social media. They can pray at any time on any day.

People can watch and share videos as often as they like. They can go back and review content they missed or seek additional information on their own. They can binge watch sermons and consume an entire year of church in one month.

There will continue to be a need to be physically present with others in worship services, but it will not need to be every week.

It is kind of like listening to music. Right now, I can listen to just about any song from any artist with just a few clicks. I do not need to go to a record store. I do not need to find out where a band is playing. Music is available to me, and I consume it more than ever. I love music more than ever. I have a greater appreciation of a wider range of music than I ever thought possible. My engagement with music has greatly increased, but my need to physically go places to experience music has decreased. I still buy records from a record store because I like to flip through the stacks from time to time. I still go to concerts and live music venues because I enjoy the experience. I just do not need to do those things as often to support my love of music.

Is it possible that people could attend church services less and love Jesus more?

We will reach more people with fewer resources.

I find it funny when people say things like, "I'll give money to missions, but I don't want the pay the church's electric bill." I kind of like the thought of paying the electric bill because I understand that we use electricity to reach people. Things like lights, air conditioning, audio/visual components and so forth are useful tools to reach people. I am happy to pay for that, but that does not change the sentiment that people are expressing.

Physical
attendance
will decrease
as engagement
increases.

We will reach more people with fewer resources.

They are sensing the reality of our situation. Churches do spend a ton of money on infrastructure and methodology that does not produce much fruit. People want the resources they give to make an impact.

My entire church life I have heard that new churches are the best way to reach new people. I believed it to be true, and maybe it was...maybe it is. But here is the deal. I have planted a church, and our church currently gives 5% of our annual budget to church planting. We actively start new churches every year, and in all those church plants over all those years there has been one constant: It is expensive!

The cost per person reached in a church plant is HIGH. I think it is still worth it. After all, it is only money, and who can put a price on the salvation of a soul? But what if we could reach a lot more people with those resources?

The Decentralized Church is changing the dynamics of church staffs. People attending less frequently means less programs are needed. Fewer programs means smaller church staffs. Smaller church staffs mean more money for other things.

I met a pastor whose church was struggling financially. He asked me for some advice, so I pressed him for some details about their budget. The amount of money they spent on payroll seemed dreadfully high to me, so I asked him how many staff members he had working for the church. He told me that they had thirty full-time employees for a church that was running about 1,000 people in attendance each week.

I shared with the pastor that our church was four times their size and that we only had twenty-five full-time employees. A worried look came over his face because I think he knew that he was wasting a lot of kingdom money on unneeded staff. He got a little defensive and said, "The staff are not all pastors…ten of them are administrative assistants."

I said: "What? You have ten administrative assistants on your staff for a church of 1,000 people! We have two administrative assistants for 4,000 people, and they both fill other roles on our staff as well."

I explained to him that times had changed. Things like cell phones, email, personal computers, digital calendars and the internet in general mean that people generally do not need assistants. He thought about it for a minute and then told me that was just how they had always done things. I asked him if their budget would work if they fired nine of their administrative assistants. He told me that was not something he was willing to consider.

People know when something is not right. They may not be able to pinpoint exactly what it is, but they generally know. Churches that waste resources because they are unwilling to change are facing hard times. We have a responsibility to utilize every kingdom resource to reach the most people in the shortest time. When less money is spent on supporting outdated infrastructure, more money is available to do other things.

That principle applies to people just as well as it applies to money. You may think that I am heartless for encouraging a pastor to fire nine administrative assistants, but I would argue the he is the cruel one for letting them stay on the payroll. Our bloated church staffs are not doing the staff members any favors. The days of hiring for growth are over. More staff members do not equate to reaching more people. In fact, it could mean the opposite. If a church has staff members that it honestly does not need, the kindest thing they can do is send those people out into the workforce where they can take the church into the world. They will be more effective in serving Jesus, and the kingdom will grow.

People will have a global view of Christianity.

Information and education allow for a broader view of the world. While it is true that Satan uses xenophobia, nationalism and all manner of ignorant nonsense in attempts to throw the Church off course, I am convinced that the Holy Spirit will prevail. Eyes

People will have a global view of Christianity.

will open to the world-wide spread of the gospel, and true followers of Jesus will eagerly embrace participation in the global Church.

There will be an increase in foreign missions. People will use vacation time and money to travel for Jesus. The missionary mindset will shift from going with the purpose of saving people to going with the purpose of worshiping with people. We will long to learn from one another and to encourage the Church as a whole. Missionary involvement will move towards partnerships that are sustained by strong relational equity. There will be fewer one-off trips that produce little more than a slideshow of memories and more lifelong relationships that connect the family of God across the globe.

Communication opens us up to a whole new world of possibilities. We can pray for one another and share resources instantly. We can see what is happening anywhere in the world through cellphone technology. We are not dependent upon news crews to capture and broadcast stories. Real relationships with real people will allow us to see what is really going on. Out of sight, out of mind will no longer be the prevailing reality.

There is also a wave of missionaries coming to the United States of America. Praise God…bring them on! The Lord knows we need all the help we can get. I recently met a missionary from Africa who planted a church in the U.S. God is using him to do more with less resources than any church-planter I have ever worked with. We are eagerly learning from him and other missionaries, so we can better reach our little corner of the world for Christ.

These relational connections and the ability to communicate and travel will strengthen the Church and allow the gospel to spread rapidly. A broader world-view will allow us to see the scriptures with fresh insight. Our perversions of the biblical text will come to light, and we will have a much richer understanding of God's love. My preaching is certainly impacted by the ability to connect globally. I am discovering many things that are commonly taught in American churches are far more cultural than biblical.

For instance, in John chapter four, Jesus has an encounter with a Samaritan woman at a well. Pastors in the U.S. regularly portray this woman as a hot-to-trot floozy. Just about every time I have ever heard this text preached, there was some reference to the woman being a social outcast and a sexual deviant. I now find this notion completely absurd and laughable. Why? Because someone I know went to Africa on a mission trip and heard a pastor there preach on that text. My friend shared with me how differently people in that culture view the Samaritan woman at the well. I remember my jaw dropping as I instantly saw the foolishness of the typical American perspective on that text.

A little history lesson can help us to understand how preachers in the U.S. came to such a perverted view of this text. We apply our cultural surroundings when reading the Bible, and that influences our understanding. Preachers often speak about the woman at the well and use the fact that she had been married five times and that the man she was with was not her husband as evidence that she was morally corrupt. That mindset is largely derived from a 20th century war on divorce.

Educational, economic and social opportunities exploded for women in the 20th century. Women could vote, go to college and have careers. World War II opened the workforce to women, and as economic opportunities increased for women so did the divorce rate. The general response from the church was to blame divorce on the moral decay of society, and sadly women who were divorced often became social outcasts.

But what was really going on?

Women were often oppressed and abused in a system that afforded little opportunity for change. When career options opened up, women could leave abusive situations and live without needing a man to bring home the bacon. Women could not only legally divorce their husbands, they could actually afford to do it, too. They were no longer as trapped, so they started getting out of awful situations. A common thought embraced by many in the church was to vilify divorcees. They were often ostracized from church and from society. The economics alone of attempting to raise a family in a single parent home on generally reduced pay compared to male counterparts, pushed many divorced women to the economic and social fringes of society.

Women who were divorced were whispered about. Women who were divorced multiple times were shunned.

Preachers applied their cultural experience to the biblical text, and generations of church goers have been subjected to a grossly wrong image of the woman at the well. This matters because it greatly impacts how we understand Jesus' conversation with her. When Jesus revealed that He knew she had been married five times and that the man she was currently living with was not her husband, He was saying "I see you." Not "I see you" in the sense of I know what a dirty, rotten sinner you are, but "I see you" in the sense of I know how brutally hard your life is.

The preacher from Africa was able to preach the text more accurately. He knew that a woman from that time and place did not have legal recourse to divorce her husband. If she had been divorced five times, it was because each husband sent her away. In other words, they kicked her out of the family. Of course, divorce was not even mentioned in the text. She could have been widowed five times. If that was the case, then I am assuming there was not a long line of suitors vying to be the sixth! The issue of the woman being with a man she was not married to does not denote a sexual relationship. That is something that preachers have read into the text. In that culture, women did not have many economic opportunities. People depended on the family structure for provision, protection and identity. The fact that she was with a man she was not married to most likely meant that she was not the woman of the house. A relative had probably brought her into his home, and she was more of a servant than a family member.

Jesus was speaking to a woman with no family of her own about joining His family. He offered her living water that she would no longer need to work for. He offered her the ability to worship in spirit and in truth without having to travel to a mountain or a temple. He offered her wholeness as a part of His family.

The more we listen to voices from other cultures, the more we will become aware of our cultural biases and have our eyes opened even more to the beauty of who Jesus is. This will increase our desire to connect across the globe and appreciate the magnitude of Jesus' Church.

There will be less division over stupid stuff.

Since the economics of the Decentralized Church are not based on organizational control, there will be greater freedom to explore, think and wrestle with ideas and theology. Healthy discourse and respectful dialogue will be enjoyable elements of a truly diversified church. People will no longer feel compelled to sign fifty-point doctrinal statements in order to be considered local church members. They will be free to enjoy the mysterious majesty of God.

Fighting over methodology will decrease as Christians experience and appreciate a broader spectrum of church expressions. The simple fact that people are not trapped in singular neighborhood churches allows us all to relax and not get our holy underwear in a bunch every time we do not personally enjoy something. Liberation from institutional control and increased opportunity to explore opens our minds to a myriad of possibilities. We are free to understand that every expression does not need to be our personal cup of tea, but every expression can have value in reaching the world for Christ.

The fluid nature of the Decentralized Church paves the way for people to move gracefully. When churches attempt to hold onto their congregations and are internally focused on retention, they make it difficult for people to leave. The harder it is for people to leave a church, the more fighting over stupid stuff. Caged animals generally become nasty or docile…neither is useful for growing God's kingdom.

There will be less
division over
stupid stuff.

Expect the
unexpected.

Expect the unexpected.

Where will the Spirit lead? Wow…God only knows.

What we do know is that it will be good. It will be better than what we could do on our own. It will require more dying to self than any of us thought possible.

The Spirit of God will blow wherever He chooses.

He will blow our minds with what He does. He will blow away our sacred cows. He will blow into every dark corner of our world.

Will you go with Him, or will you blow Him off?

eOɔ

5

get it. got it. good.

One way or another, you are going to get it.

You can get on board, get out of the way or get destroyed. The choice is yours.

The Decentralized Church is here. This is happening. A genuine move of the Holy Spirit is blossoming all over the world. Power structures and church hierarchies are crumbling as people are liberated from their clutches.

You can choose to fight against the Decentralized Church, but you will not win. You cannot win when nothing is fighting back. This is part of the beauty of what God is doing. The Decentralized Church is not fighting against previous expressions. It is not a concerted effort to bring reform to the Church. It is not a movement derived from leaders with agendas to fix what is broken. The Decentralized Church is simply the Holy Spirit moving in ordinary people in ordinary places to experience extraordinary life.

How do you fight against that?

More pointedly, why would you fight against that?

One reason is that you do not understand it. People often fight what they do not understand. They get riled up and agitated without having any real idea of what is going on. I know this happens to me. I am prone to fight against what I do not understand.

I call these my "Forest Gump Moments."

If you have never seen the movie "Forest Gump," do yourself a favor…put this book down and watch it immediately. Forest Gump is a simple guy with a pure heart who goes with the flow and ends up experiencing an epically extraordinary life. The movie ends with an image of a feather floating in the breeze. The best life any of us could ever hope to live would be one where we are light enough to float wherever the Spirit leads to experience whatever He desires.

Okay…back to my "Forest Gump Moments."

In the film, Forest doesn't always understand the changing world around him, but his simple nature allows him to experience things other people were missing out on. Forest was not book smart, but he could run fast, and he wound up getting a football scholarship to the University of Alabama. There is a scene where Forest is trying to go to class while the school is experiencing forced racial integration. Forest walked into an angry mob of students and protesters who were screaming racially-charged threats against the African American students who were being led into the school building by police.

Forest got this super-concerned look on his face as he tried to process what was going on. He could not figure out why everyone was so upset so he asked another student what was going on. The student said, "They are letting coons in the schoolhouse." (FYI… "Coons" is a derogatory and highly inappropriate reference to African American people. Forest would never think or speak this way, so he assumed the student was referring to actual raccoons.)

Pure-hearted Forest got angry and concerned too, because raccoons do not belong in a schoolhouse. He did not understand what was happening, and the tension builds as you watch Forest get sucked into the angry mob mentality. I know that feeling. I know what it feels like to encounter angry people and to fall into the mob without understanding the dynamics of the situation. In my mind, the movie freezes on Forest's indignant, incredulous face, and I know that feeling. Anger is contagious, but so is love.

Forest snapped out of his angry moment when one of the African American students dropped a book while trying to get through the mob. He helped her out by picking up the book, and then he walked into the school building with the African American students.

Forest did not dwell in the angry tension of what he did not understand. The wind blew, and he moved on. I want to live like that, so I pay close attention to what is going on when I find myself joining the angry mob. I can feel that look of confused concern come over me when I am about to fight what I do not understand. It is like I can see Forest Gump looking back at me in a mirror.

Imagine an angry mob gathering together to try to stop the Decentralized Church. What would they shout? What would be written on the signs they hold? Where would the mob gather?

That last question has a funny and revealing answer. Where would the mob gather? The answer is…online. The primary fight against this mighty move of the Holy Spirit will take place on social media, blogs and websites. Many people will join the mob and spew mean-spirited ignorance. Many more will join the fringes with concerned looks of confusion. But those who are led by the blowing of the Spirit will cut through the mob to walk into a new realm of freedom and effectiveness.

An insane amount of resources will be wasted in a totally one-sided fight. Time, energy and money will be misallocated away from winning the world for Christ and into preserving ineffective methodology. At some point, the angry mob will realize that it is just yelling at itself. Everyone else will have moved on. A remnant will be left to grieve, but the majority will have moved on into the greatest explosion of kingdom growth the world has ever seen.

> *"If you bite and devour each other, watch out or you will be destroyed by each other. So I say, walk by the Spirit, and you will not gratify the desires of the flesh. For the flesh desires what is contrary to the Spirit, and the Spirit what is contrary to the flesh. They are in conflict with each other, so that you are not to do whatever you want. But if you are led by the Spirit, you are not under the law."*
> **Galatians 5:15-18 (NIV)**

Watch out! Be on guard against fighting the wrong fight. Fighting against the movement of the Holy Spirit is like trying to fight the wind. Your punches will never land, and you will flail around until exhaustion consumes you.

The fight against the Decentralized Church is a complete waste of energy. If you are not willing to get on board, the least you could do is get out of the way. The movement will not be stopped. It will not even be slowed down. The momentum is too great. Those who try to stand in the way are going to be blown over. I do not want that to happen. God does not want that to happen. I assume that you do not want that to happen.

I desperately want you to get it. I want you to understand what God is up to with His Church. I want you to get on board with the movement of the Holy Spirit.

You may be thinking: "I get it. I just don't like it…or…I get it. I just don't agree with it."

I get it…you get it, but you don't got it.

Understanding something cognitively is not the same as embracing something holistically. A Decentralized Church makes perfect sense for fulfilling the mission of Jesus to save the world. It is a powerful way for the gospel to rapidly reach every corner of the globe as people are released from going to church, so they can be the Church. It makes sense. It is logical, rational and biblical.

But.

Yeah but.

There is always that big "but" planted in the pews of every church.

Are you ready for it?

Here we go.

"But that's not the way we have always done it!"

We must get our big "buts" out of the way so that we not only get it...we GOT it. Then the Church will be good.

There are many things about the current expressions of the Church that are not good, and the Decentralized Church is bringing renewal, reform and revival.

The systematic sexual abuse of children by clergy protected by a corrupt institutional hierarchy is NOT good. The consumer-driven mindset of the evangelical world that perverts Jesus by using His Church to promote selfishness, greed and political power is NOT good. The stagnation and acceptance of no kingdom growth found in much of our traditional expressions is NOT good. The racial segregation of local churches is NOT good. The oppression of women is NOT good. Loving outdated methods over effectiveness is NOT good. Ignoring the poor is NOT good.

All of that not good is NOT God. He is doing a new thing, and it is good because God is good.

Do you get it? Have you got it? Good.

A whole lot of good is coming fast. Here are some good things on the horizon.

People will see themselves as priests.

I find it funny how upset ordained clergy get when people go online and get themselves ordained. Professional clergy see online ordination as a threat to their powerbase. It is understandable...many ordained church leaders went through years of formal education, rigorous ordination processes and have strict denominational accountability. The fact that someone can jump online and be ordained in a matter of minutes essentially makes a mockery of the whole system.

But what is up with the system to begin with? Is a professional clergy made up of religious experts that are largely disconnected from real people in the real world what God really intended? I wonder what the early church would think of the current church's robes, rings, funky hats, clerical collars, titles, hierarchy, degrees and other religious rigmarole. It is all a goofy, top-heavy structure that is bound to topple at some point. Now is as good a time as any.

The wind blows and the hierarchy sways. TIMBER!

Empowered people are realizing that they do not need the institutionalized church. The number one reason people go online to get ordained is so that they can legally perform a wedding for a friend. Think about that for a minute. How did the church get in the wedding business to begin with? There is nothing in the New Testament about ordained clergy performing weddings. Jesus never said anything about that. These church traditions of marrying and burying...weddings and funerals...emerged as sources of power, manipulation and monetary gain.

People do not need a church for funerals or weddings. They do not need local religious experts to answer questions. They can go online to research any topic and communicate with educated people from all over the world. They do not need permission to start ministry efforts within their spheres of influence. People do not need the control of church hierarchy when they are released as ministers of the gospel.

People will see
themselves as
priests.

The priesthood of believers is a foundational element of Protestant churches, but time and tradition has eroded it as the church drifted back into the realm of power and control. It is time for a course correction. The rise and release of regular people to carry the gospel to the ends of the earth is upon us.

> *"But you are a chosen people, a royal priesthood, a holy nation, God's special possession, that you may declare the praises of him who called you out of darkness into his wonderful light."*
> **1 Peter 2:9 (NIV)**

As someone who has done the religious work of weddings and funerals, I can personally attest to the silliness of it all. Is a church wedding somehow more sacred than wedding in a park? Is it more meaningful to have a clergy member that is loosely connected to the bride and groom say some prepared religious words and then wait awkwardly to the side to take a quick photo with the couple before scampering off to attend to other religious duties or to have a family member or close friend do the job? I have sat through church funeral services that offered nothing more than jumping through some religious hoops. The real funeral happened later in a bar, restaurant or home as family and friends celebrated a life well lived and comforted one another.

People are waking up and choosing a better way. They have been preached at and told to read their Bibles, to pray daily, to serve

Jesus, to see themselves as ministers and to go into their world to do the work of the Church. Some of them listened! It has moved beyond sounding like a good idea to actually being done.

The role of church leaders in the Decentralized Church will not be to control but to continually empower and release. Do not attempt to corral what God is doing. Do not try to create systems and procedures to direct the movement of the Spirit. Simply empower and release. Help people see that they are the priesthood of believers.

The Decentralized Church will grow fastest in the most irreligious places.

Religion will fight the Decentralized Church, so the path of least resistance will be found in places that are most irreligious. People who are done with religion are not necessarily done with Jesus. Most of them are extremely open to relational connection with Jesus and are eager to experience that connection apart from the trappings of traditional religious expressions.

The Decentralized Church allows people who would never consider walking through the doors of a church building to experience worship, community and the love of God in powerfully effective ways. Religion has done some intense damage that should not be ignored. Someone who was sexually abused by a person of power

The Decentralized Church will grow fastest in the most irreligious places.

in the church is not likely to feel comfortable bringing children to a church building regardless of how safe and secure the child check-in procedures are. Someone impacted by financial scandals in the church generally is not interested in supporting traditional church infrastructure. Someone who was kicked out of church, denied communion or was shunned because of perceived sin isn't likely to risk stepping back into a church building to experience the pain all over again. People who endured false teaching, hateful rhetoric and politically motivated manipulation at the hands of local church leaders are not interested in enduring any more.

But people are still desperate for Jesus and for connection in the family of God. The Decentralized Church will flourish first in the places where the existing church has been irrelevant and ineffective the longest. The fields are ripe for harvest as there are now multitudes of people who are several generations removed from any form of active religious expression. They do not carry the baggage of Christianity as a religion and therefore feel much freer to embrace Jesus relationally.

The harvest is plentiful and so are the workers if we release people to be the Decentralized Church. Regions of the globe that have long been considered spiritually dark will burn the quickest and brightest as the Decentralized Church. Areas that religious voices have written off as being spiritually desolate will lead the way into the greatest evangelistic explosion the world has ever seen. Buckle up, butter cup, and watch what happens in places like Canada, New England and Europe.

Reform will come to existing churches.

I do not believe the Decentralized Church is a reformation movement, but a side benefit will be some needed reform in existing church expressions. The initial response by many church leaders will be attempts to control. Some will cling tighter to old methodology and teach that anything new is bad. Others will do everything in their power to maintain control over their perceived "flock."

We see this type of behavior every time God raises up a voice in His Church to speak to a larger audience. Those voices get attacked from within the Church by leaders who feel threatened. They lose some of their control as "their" people hear another voice. The response is typically to pick apart the teachings, lifestyle, background, personality and character of the person people are listening to. This is done overtly through public accusations and covertly through disparaging comments meant to subtly discredit.

This type of behavior is intolerable but is so widely accepted that many church leaders actually believe it is their duty. It is absolutely sickening the way church leaders ignorantly attack what they do not understand. It is no surprise that their minions end up doing the same thing and suddenly the internet is filled with ridiculous blogs and comments that attempt to destroy servants of Christ.

The drama and the nonsense must stop. The fear-based negativity can provide some short-term control, but the outlook is bleak for those who choose that road. Church leaders that go negative and attack will attract people who are prone to go negative and attack. Guess what those people will end up doing? Yep! They will eventually go negative and attack that leader. They will fight and destroy their local church.

Attempts to control will produce a stranglehold. The Holy Spirit will not be wrangled. He cannot be contained. Churches will either choke themselves out and die or repent and release people to freely be the Church. It will be interesting to see how denominations and more liturgical church expressions creatively navigate preserving traditional expressions of worship while releasing control. Decisions will need to be made regarding what truly is nonnegotiable.

Churches will need to be clearer on the "whys" behind their practices. Rote, religious duties will not have much of an appeal, but if genuine meaning is expressed through ancient practices there will always be people who migrate towards connections with the past. The Decentralized Church does not mark the end of traditional church expressions but perhaps a new beginning.

Reform will come to existing churches.

The crazy messiness of the Decentralized Church will magnify the desires in some to have a sturdier footing in their worship experiences. Existing churches that refrain from negatively attacking new expressions, that make strategic decisions about what is sacred and simply explain why they do what they do will effectively meet a need in the emerging church world.

God will use the Decentralized Church to help provide some course corrections for existing church methodologies. This is great news! Any church can get a little "off" over time. Missional drift by only a degree or two sets a course for disaster as you move further away from your intended destination with each passing year. The movement of the Holy Spirit will lift up the heads of church leaders to survey the changing landscape. They will ask tough questions. Who are we? What are we doing? What should we do? Are we on course? What can change?

Churches that resist fear and honestly evaluate these important questions will make some changes and continue the mission of Jesus to save the world.

Do you get it? Have you got it? Can you see that it is good?

၈၀၁

6

the great equalizer

Who is the Decentralized Church?

Everyone. Young and old. Rich and poor. Urban, suburban and rural. Conservative and liberal. Male and female. All races and nationalities. The Decentralized Church is a brilliant kaleidoscope of God's creation.

The family of God is finally experiencing the promise of scripture.

"So in Christ Jesus you are all children of God through faith, for all of you who were baptized into Christ have clothed

yourselves with Christ. There is neither Jew nor Gentile, neither slave nor free, nor is there male and female, for you are all one in Christ Jesus. If you belong to Christ, then you are Abraham's seed, and heirs according to the promise."

Galatians 3:26-29 (NIV)

As people spend more time online, distinctions such as race, gender, age, social status and formal education will become less important. You can be whoever you want to be online. People who are typically meek can be bold. People who have never had a platform or a voice can express themselves. The anonymity of sitting in front of a keyboard provides a realm that feels safe to explore thoughts, feelings and identities that would otherwise remain suppressed.

Since online is the real world, does that make an online persona reality? As people spend more time online, they cling less to physical distinctions. Things like age, race and gender are fairly meaningless online. We warn children that if they think they are chatting online with a twelve-year old girl that it is probably a forty-year old man. The internet provides an infinite number of ways for people to sin, but it also provides an infinite number of ways for people to glorify God.

Identity confusion in the midst of our online world is not surprising. People are not necessarily bouncing back and forth from the online and physical realms…we are combining the two. The combination effect prevents us from viewing the online world as fantasy because there are physical-world consequences to online actions and online consequences for physical world actions.

The lines of social distinctions are blurred. It is more difficult to define and generalize people based on traditional categories because people see themselves differently. Traditional church methodology is based on reaching distinct groups of people. This becomes increasingly ineffective as people no longer see themselves in segregated social circles.

Diversity is a beautiful thing, but the existing church continually takes measures to ensure that people remain as segregated as possible. The chosen methodology for just about everything churches do reinforces social segregation.

The seeker-sensitive movements of the 1980s and 90s taught churches to identify their target audience. Churches all over the United States actually created profiles of who they were trying to reach. These profiles included things like age, ethnicity, education, income, family dynamics and religious preferences. Churches then built their methodology around catering to the profiles they created. This activity produced a short-term boom in growth as churches moved out of the realm of boring irrelevance into strategic initiatives, but the long-term impact reinforced segregationist programing.

Our world is becoming increasingly integrated, but churches for the most part are not adapting. Fixed geographic locations, styles of music, preaching techniques, clothing, manners of speech and programs all tend to cater to segregated groups. It is no accident that churches are the most racially segregated organizations in the United States. This travesty has happened on purpose as churches refused to change methodology and embrace the positive social change in the culture around them.

I was speaking at a Christian conference, and as usual, I noticed that most of the room I was talking to was eerily similar to me… white, middle-aged, college-educated, professional men. There was some diversity present but not a whole lot. It was more like the kind of diversity that sticks out instead of blending in. When my session was over, there was some social time for people to interact, but I was not all that eager to shoot the breeze about the same old topics, so I decided to go to the restaurant next door to grab a bite to eat by myself.

When I walked into the restaurant, I spoke to a gentleman who was waiting to be seated. I recognized him from the group I was speaking to because he was part of the conspicuous diversity. To be clear, he was a black dude. He too had left the room because he was not particularly interested in listening to the same old people talk about the same old stuff. I asked him to join me for dinner, and he agreed.

We hit it off fast. We liked much of the same music, movies, books and comedians. We were laughing and having a great time. We joked about the lack of diversity in the organization I was speaking to, and he started to open up about his experiences as one of the only black guys in the room.

I asked him what he thought we could do to make things better. His response kind of surprised me. He said he did not know because his experiences in all-black churches were pretty similar to my experiences in all-white churches. He expressed frustration at how his church would publicly say that they wanted diversity, but their actions actively prevented it. He told me about an interracial couple that attended his church that was gossiped about and essentially ostracized. He said his church did not want white people attending.

I said, "Come on, man…I could come to your church. They would LOVE me!"

He said, "Oh…you could visit, but you couldn't STAY!"

Wow. This is what much of our church methodology has produced. A mentality that conveys that people who are different are welcome to visit, but they can't stay. It makes no sense. Segregation is not the nature of Jesus, and it should never be the nature of His Church. Things are horrifically wrong.

And it is not just racial segregation. Churches do it with age, economic status, educational experience and family dynamics.

Consider how many churches try to best minister to their people. They often split them into segregated, homogenous groups. Kids go to the children's ministry. Students go to the youth ministry. Young adults have their group. Single people have theirs. Don't forget the old people. Every church needs a Seasoned Saints group, right?

Maybe not. There are clearly times when grouping people together according to their stage of life is appropriate, but when that becomes the prevailing mentality, there is a richness of diversity that is lost.

Here is a great idea…let's get a bunch of young parents together who have little kids and have no idea what they are doing. They are tired of their own kids and certainly do not want to deal with anybody else's kids. Let's put these young parents and all their children into a small group and have them meet in somebody's home. Chaos and destruction will ensue. There will be amplified crying and whining…and that's just what's coming from the dads…the kids are another story entirely. This is often not a life-giving situation. But what if those parents were connected to empty nesters and unmarried adults? They could get life-giving advice and assistance. Diversity helps alleviate problems; segregation often exacerbates problems.

When I was in college, there were two large churches in town that had huge college ministries. Whenever I met people on campus, they would inquire as to which of the two churches I attended. They were shocked when I told them that I was part of a church that did not have many college students. I explained that I lived with college students, interacted all day with college students and had many built-in social outlets to connect with college students. What I did not have was connections with older and younger people.

I will admit that I am tired of all the books, conferences and blogs about how to reach generations X,Y,Z…millennials, boomers and whatever other labels we want to paste on people. Often when a church makes a concerted effort to reach one particular group, they wind up alienating another group. There is a tug and pull that creates tension, and then nobody is really enjoying the church. And when nobody is enjoying the church, there is no joy in the church. Joyless churches do not reach people with the gospel. They are lifeless, empty and utterly unattractive.

As I experience more of the Decentralized Church, I am loving how we are free to appreciate and embrace people who are different. Since we are not in competition for resources (building space, attention from pastoral staff, budget dollars, stylistic preferences and so forth), we are open to connect across cultural barriers. One of the greatest benefits of this move of the Holy Spirit is that churches that allow for decentralized expressions will be free from trying to cater to consumers. These churches can get on with the business of Jesus to save the world. The fruit of their labors will be more people in the kingdom of heaven, and this will produce a contagious and attractive joy.

People are thinking differently. The old are staying young at heart. The young are wise beyond their years. The flow of information and the connectivity that the internet provides is rapidly broadening our world-view. We have the ability to interact with a variety of voices every day. The increased awareness of one another creates a deep appreciation in some and a deep fear in others. Some people run to embrace diversity, and some dig their heels in to destroy diversity.

Heel diggers want things to stay the same, but things are not the same.

The wind blows.

The Spirit comes.

Everything changes.

Existing infrastructures and hierarchies resist these changes because they do not fit into their traditional models and methods. Traditional expressions of church will fight to suppress emerging voices in attempts to maintain control. But Jesus is the great Equalizer! His Spirit is moving, and His voice will resound in and through the Decentralized Church.

People who have never understood the good news of Jesus will hear it in fresh ways that they can finally process and receive. People who have been told to sit down, shut up and blindly submit will stand up, speak up and lead others to freedom.

> *"In the last days, God says,*
> *I will pour out my Spirit on all people.*
> *Your sons and daughters will prophesy,*
> *your young men will see visions,*
> *your old men will dream dreams.*
> *Even on my servants, both men and women,*
> *I will pour out my Spirit in those days,*
> *and they will prophesy.*
> *I will show wonders in the heavens above*

and signs on the earth below,
blood and fire and billows of smoke.
The sun will be turned to darkness
and the moon to blood
before the coming of the great and glorious day of
the Lord.
And everyone who calls
on the name of the Lord will be saved."

Acts 2:17-21 (NIV)

These are our last days. The end is near. Time is short. The Spirit is being poured out on all people.

Everyone who calls on the name of the Lord will be saved. Everyone. Everyone. Everyone. Everyone. Everyone. Everyone. Everyone.

Everyone who calls on the name of the Lord will receive His Spirit. Everyone. Everyone. Everyone. Everyone. Everyone. Everyone. Everyone.

Everyone who calls on the name of the Lord will have a voice. Everyone. Everyone. Everyone. Everyone. Everyone. Everyone. Everyone.

Everyone who calls on the name of the Lord will have a place and purpose in His Church. Everyone. Everyone. Everyone. Everyone. Everyone. Everyone. Everyone.

For everyone who has found out that the deck is stacked against them, the cards are getting shuffled, and a new hand is being dealt. Game on.

∽

BONUS CHAPTER

(for pastors only)

7

the cursed back door

Releasing the church to be the Church is a paradigm shift. Much of a pastor's training and experience revolves around keeping sheep in a pen, but sheep in pens are completely incapable of reaching the world for Christ. Books, conferences, blogs and training regularly encourage pastors to focus on closing the back door of their churches.

The Decentralized Church says, "Forget the back door...knock down the back wall."

Insane amounts of resources are regularly wasted in attempts to retain what ought to be released.

Many churches take an inward turn by attempting to hold onto what they believe to be theirs. We forget that the Church belongs to Jesus. We are His body. We are His people. We are His servants.

Jesus can move us anywhere He wants anytime He wants. Focused retention effort reallocates resources away from reaching out, and we wind up simply trying to hold on.

I met with the leadership of a church that was thinking about closing their doors after almost 40 years of ministry. They were agonizing over their dwindling church. Average weekly attendance had dipped to around fifty, and the financial situation was bleak. The leadership was frustrated, exhausted and afraid.

I asked if they knew why their church was dying, and the Senior Pastor quickly spoke up. He explained how the last twelve months had been the perfect storm. He shared that ten families had left the church, and he felt that if those families were still there, everything would be fine.

I asked if they knew why the ten families had left the church. The pastor listed the reasons: two families had job transfers, one family got divorced, one moved into a nursing home, two went to another local church that had programing for children, one got married and started attending her husband's church, one had to start working on Sundays, one went to be a worship leader at another church, and one passed away.

The pastor reiterated that if those ten families were still there, everything would be fine. I told them that their problem was not that ten families left their church. Their problem was that twenty new families had not started worshiping with them.

There will always be people that leave, and most of the time they leave for normal reasons…life change, job relocation or a felt need that is better met elsewhere. I left a great church in Texas to be a part of a great church in New Hampshire. It is wrong to try to retain people when we ought to release people.

Holding on for dear life is no good. It produces a survival mentality and a scarcity mindset. Many of the issues rampant in local church expressions are derived from survival mode.

Survival mode produces a fear-based ministry approach. "Be afraid. Be very afraid." This becomes the mantra of churches that are merely holding on. They fear the world and all the "evil" people "out there." They fear other churches and actively attempt to diminish the work those churches do in order to keep their flock from experiencing those things. They fear anything new because survival mode has no time or energy for innovation. Fear spreads like wildfire and devours curiosity and experimentation.

Fear cannot handle being questioned, challenged or confronted. A fearful church will produce an angry church.

Angry churches are ugly. Yes U-G-L-Y…they ain't got no alibi. They ugly.

Anger is unattractive. It is repulsive to those who are not already angry. Anger runs contrary to the basic nature of Jesus and His Church. Angry churches are actively fighting against Jesus. YIKES!

It is pretty easy to spot anger from the outside, but it is brutally tough to recognize when you are in it. Anger is a massive blind spot for most who are angry. Think about it. Has anyone ever told you not to be mad? How did you respond? Most of us wind up screaming, "I'm **not** MAD!"

An angry church will preach about what they are against instead of what they are for. There is rarely any good news in their worship services, ministry efforts or daily living. Most of their time is spent finger-pointing, complaining and building walls to protect themselves from the evil world out there.

Angry churches are hyper-critical. They pick apart everything in Christian culture. They can tell you where various authors, pastors and theologians are wrong in their theology. They know which translation of the Bible is most accurate and why it is the only one anyone should ever read. They can tell you what is wrong with every other local church and why it would be dangerous to worship with those people.

Fear-based, angry churches become defensive.

There is a need to defend their turf. A territorial mindset takes over. You will start to hear phrases like "stealing sheep" in reference to people going to different churches. Stealing sheep? Are you kidding me? They are not your sheep. People belong to Jesus, and if He wants to move His sheep around to different pastures so they can grow and be used in new ways, then that is His business. One of the worst things a church could ever do is attempt to hold onto someone that God is leading away. It is cruel, confusing and crippling.

The church ought to be constantly releasing and sending, but our defensiveness destroys any hope for vision. We build ministry walls to keep people in, and by default the same walls keep new people out. This grieves the heart of God, and the defensive efforts do not even work for their intended purpose. People still leave—we just make it harder and more hurtful. It takes them a bit longer to find a way out, and they typically get hurt on the way. It is like they are escaping from prison. They have to tunnel under the walls for years, scale a giant fence, navigate barbed wire and hope that they don't get shot in the back.

Seriously. So many people have stories about church that start with, "I got burned in my last church." They should have been released and sent with a blessing, but instead were cursed with immense baggage from a fearful, angry and defensive church.

Defensive churches will die. It is a simple, logical fact. Maintenance mode is death mode. Survival mode only delays the inevitable. All of the efforts to protect their little slice of the kingdom lead to its dwindling into nothingness. Holding onto people who ought to be released and sent chokes the life out of them. They may give up, lay down and tamely stay put, but there will be no life in them. Most dying churches have actually been dead for so long that you can smell the stench of rot and decay from miles away.

Control is a symptom of defensiveness. In order to defend our turf, we need to control everyone. We need control over their time, money, activities and thoughts. In order to accomplish this, controlling churches are mega-busy with programs and activities designed to circle the wagons and keep everybody in. The church calendar is a big deal because it has members' social lives planned out for them. People in controlling churches never have friends who do not know Jesus and almost never have friends who attend a different church. How could they? They are wrapped up in the controlling, sterile environment of their defensive, angry, fear-based subculture.

Fear-based, angry churches become defensive.

Guilt and manipulation are two of the greatest tools used for control. A church has crossed a dangerous line into the realm of control when it starts to wield these tools. People in a controlling church environment will often apologize for missing a church service or activity. Why would they feel compelled to do that? I think it is because they know they have offended the church by not being there. The only reason the church would be offended is if they have taken a defensive posture. Guilt flows from that type of thinking.

"Where were you? You should have been here. We really missed you. What were you doing that was more important than church? How dare you have a life outside of our control!"

Manipulation follows on guilt's heels.

"If you love Jesus, then church must be a priority. You really let us all down when you are not here. Our church is struggling, and it is your fault for not being more committed."

Churches wind up holding people hostage. People are manipulated to stay when they really want to go. The church experience becomes miserable for them and miserable people make for miserable churches. Miserable churches repulse new people.

When people do manage to escape the hostage situation, the leadership typically speaks negatively about them and whatever new church they may be attending. I warn pastors all the time about this nasty behavior. Churches that badmouth people who leave and attack other ministries and pastors are doomed. The only people that they will attract are other negative, mean-spirited people. When they run out of people to attack, they turn on each other and rip each other apart. Their destruction is imminent but not quick enough. These churches often hang on for a long time on their slow march towards death, and in the interim, they give Jesus a bad name.

In 2004, we started a new church in a North Dallas, Texas suburb. It was a fast-growing community with a ton of potential for outreach. It was an amazing place to build a new local church, but we arrived just a little too late. There was a wave of church-planters that arrived three years ahead of us that were already building their first facilities when we arrived on the scene. Every church in the area that built a building grew from 300 to 1,000 in weekly attendance overnight.

Our church was part of twelve other new church starts that took over the temporary spaces (schools, movie theaters, etc.) that the more "established" churches left behind. It sounds a bit crazy, but twelve new churches started in this suburb within one year of our launch. It is an understatement to say that we were saturated with new churches. The new churches never had much of a chance. After four years, our church was the only one left, and that was only because we had financial backing from a large church across town.

We found that we could reach a certain demographic of people that did not feel welcomed in established churches. They were welcomed. I knew these churches. These churches loved Jesus and loved people. They were not judgmental or exclusionary. However, there were people who at some point had a negative experience with church and would walk into a public elementary school for a worship service that would never walk through the doors of a church building. We focused our efforts on finding and reaching those people.

It was exciting at first, but then after six months or a year, these people would decide that they needed to go to one of the more established churches. Conventional wisdom told us to hunt them down and try to keep them. These efforts were worse than fruitless…they were damaging. I personally laid on the guilt and manipulated people into staying. They were miserable and ended up eventually leaving anyway.

How do you process that dynamic? You love on people who feel rejected by established churches. You help them connect to God. You walk with them through their issues and help them be healed and whole. Then they want to go to another church!

What do you do with that?

I started asking these questions, and what I found out was that God was leading these people to different places. At first, I was afraid and angry and defensive and controlling, but after a while I realized that they needed to go. It was best for them to go. However, ministry training told me that I was supposed to do everything in my power to keep these people in MY FLOCK!

Ugh. Yuck. How pathetic can you get?

I was afraid. I was losing my church. People were going to "better" churches. Yep…BETTER!

Some went to churches that had recovery programs. Some went to churches that had active student ministries. Some went to churches that had divorce care. God led these wonderful, precious children of His to places where they could experience healing and be more effective in building His kingdom.

What kind of anti-Christ would I be if I tried to stop them? Why would I stop them?

As pathetic as this is to confess…I need to tell you that I was actively competing with other churches, and it was all my fault.

Holding people hostage is sinful. Send them with a blessing. Encourage them. Release them. Stop competing with other ministries and recognize what is truly at stake.

Hold loosely to your local church and tightly to Jesus and His kingdom.

Ultimately, there is only one name that matters, and that name is not the name of your local church. It is the name of Jesus. It is His Church. All of these silly little buildings, church names, hierarchies and denominations will pass away. None of them will remain. Jesus and His kingdom are all that matter.

Are you releasing people to build Christ's kingdom or controlling them to build yours?

The amount of resources that are allocated to extending the lives of dying churches is heart-wrenching. The misallocation of these kingdom resources is not only wasteful, it is destructive. We are destroying people, families and communities by investing in fruitless endeavors. People who are knowledgeable and interested in reaching the world for Christ become frustrated with the absurdity of it all.

It is not just dying churches that are wasting resources and damaging people. People need to be able to leave healthy, growing churches with blessings instead of curses. I have been super fortunate to be a part of healthy churches that were reaching new people and significantly impacting their communities with the love of Jesus, but even in those environments, certain voices would rise up within the leadership proclaiming that we needed to shut the back door.

These voices would regularly discount outreach, growth and anything new that God was doing because we had people sneaking out the back door. The biggest issue for most of these voices was that their church looked different than it used to. This crazy thing called "change" was happening all of the time. Growth and change are terrifying for people who desperately need control.

Don't get me wrong, the voices make arguments that sound super-Jesusy and uber-spiritual. They express that shepherds must protect the flock, and we need to locate every lost sheep. Well...I am all about finding lost sheep. The problem is that most of the people who leave churches are not lost. We are taking our seeking-and-saving energies and misapplying them to people who are already saved and are not lost or confused.

Many times over the years, I participated in tracking down people who were sneaking out the back door of our church to try to lure them back. I would meet them and ask questions. "Why are you leaving? What are you looking for? Is there anything we could do differently to make you stay?" FYI...this is God-awful leadership.

I can be a pretty persuasive guy, and generally I could convince them to come back to our church. Sadly, I am all too capable of laying on the guilt and manipulation when it suits me. We would agree to change things they didn't like, and we would work toward trying to be like whatever church they were looking for.

This **never** works. It merely delays the inevitable and throws your church off the trajectory God has you on. People would come back and suck it up for another six months, but they were miserable. Their hearts were not with us. They wanted to be somewhere else. Most importantly, God probably wanted them somewhere else.

God can reallocate His resources whenever He wants. He calls people to different churches to use them how He desires. We are ignorant fools when we think that our little, local church expression is the be-all, end-all in the Church. Holding onto people that God is calling elsewhere has hellish consequences.

Think about how many people we have cursed by preventing them from being where God desires. We want to shut the back door, so we convince people to suck it up and stick it out. Their misery increases because they are not where God wants them to be. Their negativity increases. It spreads. The entire church becomes miserable. Miserable churches do not reach new people. The people we are holding onto still want to go, but now they must make a scene when they exit. When the back door is locked, bolted, chained and nailed shut, people must make some significant noise in order to get out!

When they do manage to escape, they are damaged. We put them into positions where they would be more likely to sin and be divisive. Sin takes its toll on people. Their negativity and misery cause them to question if they could ever be useful in a church. They escape after six months of holding on, but then they are exhausted and need another six months to recuperate. Then they need another six months to determine where God might use them, and it takes six months after that to get connected and actually begin to trust another church. Our crazy backdoor thinking regularly puts people out of commission for two years. That is unacceptable.

The church that I am a part of is large. We have thousands who worship with us every week. We utilize hundreds of volunteers across our campuses to have worship services. We are always recruiting and training new volunteers, but here is the truth—we do not have a spot for everyone. GASP!

Let's pretend that you are a drummer. You are a decent drummer…rhythmically gifted…emerging in the percussive arts. You are a part of our church, and you have a growing desire to serve Jesus with your musical passion. You observe five different drummers that volunteer on our worship team, and you are impressed with how good they all are. You imagine what it would be like to play drums on a worship team, and you wonder if you are good enough to play with our team.

You probably are not.

Stick with me…don't get defensive…remember that this is a hypothetical situation.

Our worship teams are really good, and the drummer must be excellent in order to keep up and contribute. We pull from a talent pool of thousands and thousands of people. Excellent musicians enjoy playing with other excellent musicians, so our worship ministry attracts some amazing talent.

If you aren't sure whether you are a good enough drummer to play with the team, it is highly unlikely that you are. We could work with you and help you develop and grow. Over time, you might work your way into the drumming rotation. Or you might simply sit in the auditorium air drumming and day-dreaming about serving Jesus week after week.

But…what if there is a church down the road that is praying for a drummer just like you?

What if God is calling you to serve in a different local church? What if God has plans to use you and to put you into play for His mission to save the world?

You should go. You should be sent. You should be sent as a blessing to another church.

Hold up. There is just one problem.

The back door.

How do you get out without causing damage? Can you leave without criticizing the church? Can you go without a ton of negative baggage? The back door generally causes people to believe and say hurtful things. "My church didn't want me. They are all about putting on a big show. It is just too big to care about real people. They wouldn't use me. They rejected me."

Curses.

Knock down that cursed back door. In fact, blow up the back wall.

The church ought to be a fluid movement of people coming in and going out. We receive and send.

Churches do not need walls. Knock them down. Let people in and let them leave. Even better…pull them in and send them out. Send them with blessing and purpose.

Send people wherever God will use them to reach the most people in the shortest time.

People often have vision, passion and ability for specific ministries that, for whatever reason, the church they are a part of is not going to utilize. These people should not be held onto. They should be sent.

Sometimes people need to be in a bigger or smaller context. Great! Send them.

Sometimes people need to come back. Great! Welcome them.

The harder we make it for people to go, the harder it will be for them to come back.

Blow up that cursed back wall, and set the Church free!

∽

About the Author

Bo Chancey is the Senior Pastor of Manchester Christian Church in New Hampshire. He is a gifted communicator who is passionate about challenging people to fall madly in love with Jesus Christ and believes that God desperately desires all people to find the freedom of living an abundant life in Him.

Bo received a degree in History and Speech Communications at Texas A&M University. He and his wife, Somer, have three children: Alizah, Aysen and Ensley. Bo enjoys sports, working creatively, spending time with his family and preaching.

For more information, visit bochancey.com.